A Celebration of Spring

DAVID ADAM

SPCK

Published in Great Britain in 2005 by
Society for Promoting Christian Knowledge
36 Causton Street
London SW1P 4ST

British Library Cataloguing-in-Publication Data
A catalogue record for this book is available from the British Library.

ISBN 0–281–05701–X

1 3 5 7 9 10 8 6 4 2

Designed and typeset by Monica Capoferri
Printed in Belgium

INTRODUCTION

Spring is a time for wonder, for change, for growth and renewal: it is a time when hearts and earth are warmed. The long cold nights give way to brighter days and the spirit stirs. We come out from our places of protection and shelter to enjoy the refreshing air and the brightness. As the days lengthen and the sun strengthens, we seem to gain new courage and the desire to get out and achieve things. All our senses are retuned to the colours, the sounds, the tastes and smells that are about us. We enjoy the warm touch of the world upon us. This is a call to celebrate life in its fullness, to show that we are still alive!

Spring is the time of resurrection, when the dead come back to life, when that which was buried rises through the bare earth. With this comes the thrill of seeing the first of the spring flowers, the return of migrant birds and the sound of the cuckoo. New life awakens. If we are not touched by spring, we have let something within us die or allowed our hearts to become cold. There are some people who appear never to have been touched by the spring. They live in a cold climate with their abilities and attitudes frozen. Something prevents them from blossoming and their lives from flowering. Such lives lack the radiance and the fullness that should be theirs by right of birth. Sometimes an event in their lives has caused this coldness and they are afraid of being touched by warmth or change. In them, spring waits to be recognized and celebrated.

This book is an invitation to come out of the cold world and to enjoy the freshness and warmth of the new day, to let spring touch your life. In *The Selfish Giant* by Oscar Wilde we are told of a garden where spring never comes. The giant is too selfish to let anyone share his garden, so he lives in the cold lifeless world of winter. But somehow children manage to get into the garden and with them comes the spring. The giant realizes his selfishness and opens his garden and his heart to all. New warmth enters his life and surroundings. From now on he will enjoy the garden in all its seasons. He has discovered that winter was only spring asleep with the flowers resting. With the coming of spring a mighty change has come upon him and his world.

We experience all the seasons in our lives. We go through many winters and springs. Sometimes the way is dull and cheerless yet we have the ability to turn towards the light. Even in the darkest days, through faith, we can be assured that spring will return. We can walk in the light and love of our God. I know many struggling people who have spring in their hearts and the light of a new dawn in their eyes. I see people surviving great storms because they know they are not alone and that they are loved. These are resurrection people who carry Easter and spring in their whole being.

The celebration of spring is a rejoicing in our God, who makes all things new. Here is an opportunity to let the light into our lives, to allow our hearts to be warmed.

WAITING FOR SPRING

I wait for the spring to come
When frozen hearts will be warmed
And rigid attitudes will bend

I wait for the spring to come
When hidden talent will flower
And bare-boned lives will blossom

I wait for the spring to come
When darkened minds will see the light
And dull eyes will be filled with brightness

I wait for the spring to come
When we awake from the sleep of death
And arise to the joy of life immortal

PRAYER FOR LENT

Lord, the wilderness is in me
I suffer hunger and thirst
I feel a deep deprivation
I have unsatisfied longings

I want provisions for my body
Daily bread, something savoury
I need to fill the emptiness
I am hollowed out and waiting

I desire action to uplift my spirit
To raise me from this darkness
A troop of angels would do it
Or a single one to lift me up

I require stimulus to fill my mind
Stop its barren wandering
A few bright lights, a win or two
A chance to take the controls

You want me to be still
Empty, making room for you
To hunger and thirst for you
To be filled by you and your love

You want me to trust in you
And not to tempt Providence
To put my hand in yours
And not be afraid of the dark

You require me to give myself
To you and to doing your will
I am to seek your kingdom
To long and look for you

Lord, life is not wilderness
It is the start of a love affair
You have hollowed me out
To fill me fully with yourself

I rejoice now in this emptying
I await patiently your outpouring
I look for the desert to blossom
For my whole life to be God-filled

In our daily routine it is good to find a way of making a 'lifting place'. This place is our own 'holy place', where we turn in wonder and awe to refresh the day and ourselves. There is a point in the Communion service when the bread and wine are raised: it is known as the Elevation. We should all have points of elevation in our lives that raise us up above the routine of living. We need to provide ourselves with images, music, art and events that will uplift us and we must make the effort to do this. Likewise, we need to recognize that some people and relationships are uplifting. Whenever I spent the day visiting the ill and depressed, I tried to end my visits by going to see someone who was a joy to meet and an encouragement.

If we are aware of what is going on around us, there is always plenty to lower our spirits or to uplift us. We must make sure that the depressing and wearisome do not take us over completely.

I love the changing seasons. No matter what is going on, I choose to enjoy the summer days, to notice the colours of the autumn and to thrill at the first snows. Spring is special, more so after a long, hard winter. I then seek to notice the first lambs and the rising of the skylark. I never cease to rise with the lark! Often I fail to see the bird but the song on the air is such a joy. For me, wherever a lamb is born or a lark rises is a point of elevation.

A FRIDAY QUESTION

I found a lamb slain on the road
One cold dark gloomy Friday
It lay there in its own blood
And no one bothered to move it

A hawk-like shadow darkened a field
Another cold dark gloomy Friday
In the spin of death Hiroshima reeled
And no one was able to save it

A rough-hewn tree shadowed it all
One cold dark gloomy Friday
A voice to heaven did yell and call
And no one cared to answer it

My God, my God, tell me why
Why on a cold dark gloomy Friday
Men, women and lambs do die
Is there no one able to alter it?

MY FIRST SPRING

I was not prepared for this
The sunburst and green leaf
Colour and life out of the earth
The sweetness of bird song
The vernal scent of spring
I had seen pictures of flowers
I had read all their labels
I could recite their names
But I had not been touched
Not moved by their life
Nor dazzled by their brightness
My heart blossomed with delight
Tears of joy filled my eyes
Every fibre of my being thrilled
Here was life in abundance
From a fecund and fertile earth
No word could capture this
No one could press it on a page
Or ensnare it with a camera
Here creation arose before me
Celebrating life in its fullness
I stood silently in awe and rapture
At the miracle of my first spring

The first time I watched my uncle prune his roses, I looked on in horror. He seemed to be destroying good strong plants. Every snip of the secateurs diminished the plant. There was soon more on the rubbish heap than left in the ground. My uncle explained that this would make for healthier and stronger roses the following year. He also said: 'Pruning them now will protect them from being knocked about by the winter winds. This cutting back is for their own good.'

Years later, I watched the gamekeepers 'burning off' the heather on the moors. The flames attracted me. The heather was perishing in the flames; it hissed as it was burning. These countrymen knew what they were doing; all was planned and under control. The area for burning off was chosen carefully. The heather there had become old and useless, all twisted and gnarled: it had lost its sweetness and no longer sustained the moorland life. So it perished in the flames. The gamekeepers made sure the peaty soil did not burn. For a year or so after the fire, the earth was blackened and lifeless. Then, the following spring, new shoots began to show. The heather had not been destroyed, only its old body. Under the peaty soil life revived: the heather would return fresh, green and full of sustenance. It had not perished but rose like a phoenix from the flames and blackened earth. Here for me was an image of the resurrection. The old body had been destroyed, yet it did not perish – it rose again to newness of life.

As a young child, I was an avid cinema-goer. I went at least three times a week. I saw films about 'the living dead'. I began to fear being made into a zombie, one of those creatures that had life sucked out of them. When I came to live near Whitby in the 1960s, I was reminded of all this through the town's link with Bram Stoker and the novel *Dracula*. It was hard to persuade people that Dracula did not exist. They often pestered the vicar of Whitby, looking for Dracula's grave. Dracula is a fictional character, but I still fear the possibility of becoming one of the living dead.

Albert Einstein said:

'Whoever is devoid of the capacity of wonder, whoever remains unmoved, whoever cannot contemplate or know the deep shudder of the soul in enchantment might just as well be dead for he has already closed his eyes upon life.'[1]

A similar thought from Dag Hammarskjöld:

'God does not die on the day when we cease to believe in a personal deity, but we die on the day when our lives cease to be illuminated by the steady radiance, renewed daily, of a wonder, the source of which is beyond all reason.'[2]

Throughout our lives we need to keep alive the sense of awe and wonder. We need to be able to thrill at a glorious sunset, the birth of a child or the coming of a new day. Spring is a time when it is so easy to become enraptured with the sound of the cuckoo or the first flowers that appear. In the same way, we should have enjoyed the first snow, the summer heat and the colours of autumn. We need to respect the mystery and individuality of all whom we meet, and to enjoy the encounters. It is good to make sure we keep all our senses alive and do not let them die or atrophy through lack of use.

1 Quoted by Michael Mayne in *This Sunrise of Wonder*, Fount, 1995, p. 109
2 *Markings*, Faber & Faber, 1964, p. 64

CUTHBERT

Cuthbert teaches us at school
Asking us to care for the eiders
Telling us to look out for angels
He wanders through our estates
Giving streets and houses his name
He weeps that life is so trivial
He cries for the loss of wilderness
Stones on the moor bear his imprint
Crags on the Wall tell of his presence
He walks our lanes and highways
Inviting us to join in his praises
Out in the open air giving glory
No church mouse this man of God
Full of life, wanting us to pause awhile
He shares in celebrating Communion
One with us, and Christ our Saviour
Cuthbert, mighty one for God, rejoicing
Sharing in our time and in eternity

All the seasons have something to offer; this is as true for the seasons of life as of the year. Each time has its own gifts and uniqueness. One of the great arts in life is to recognize which season we are in and to enjoy it. We have to become more sensitive to our surroundings, to be aware of what is going on within us and around us. Occasionally, to appreciate where we are, we need to move to some other place: sometimes we need to move away altogether. Too often we can take our surroundings and the people about us for granted. Like the seasons, people and places change. Let us seek out each day's newness and freshness. Every day has something to offer that we have not experienced, and it asks us to break our routine even if only for a moment. Spring especially asks us to see its verdancy and to rejoice in the new day.

ROAD TO GLORY

He ignores the buzzard's cries
And sets his face to Jerusalem
Look deeply into his eyes
See the sorrow and the pain
His hands are hardened
He has worked long with wood
His feet are toughened
Walking miles of dusty roads
There is nothing in his pockets
No sword hanging at his side
He is a tramp more than a king
He has never owned anything
The ass treads on palm leaves
As they enter the Holy City
A moment of bright glory
Before the dark cloud comes
He receives a hearty welcome
Before savage rejection and pain
He cannot turn back or run
For it is for this that he came
He will be cruelly brought down
Then raise us with him to glory

SNOW ON GOOD FRIDAY

What a blasted day!
Over night young shoots frosted
Cut down by the savage icy wind
And now being buried in snow

The flowers I watched grow
Tender shoots harming no one
Deprived of life in a moment
Now all broken and flattened

I do not want to take it personally
But I find it all frustrating, annoying
A waste of my time and attention
Destruction that does not make sense

Yet on Good Friday, it happened to you
Life broken, poured out, ended
Buried in the ground, like some seed
And you came again, undefeated

Let not the coldness triumph over us
Let not the darkness or bitterness destroy us
Lord, that was cast down, uplift us
Help us rise above this, and to life eternal

The human body is a strange and mysterious thing, vibrant with energy and ever changing. Throughout its earthly existence, the body dies and rises again many times and yet the person to whom that body belongs continues. Every single cell carries the entire instructions for a hundred thousand genes. Every minute about a million cells die in our body and are replaced by another million. In the time you take to read this page, your body will have gone through many deaths and resurrections and yet you survive. You are a living miracle. New life is forever blossoming within you. I have no difficulty in believing, if God could design us this way, He could give us the power to rise again and again and give us eternal life.

AWAKENING

Dawn, birds rejoice
Rooks call resurrection
Not a thought or fear
Shaking of my winding sheet

Rooks ring out again
Tearing open the morn
Heralding the sun's journey
With the incarnate light

Sheep shake off sleep
New sounds upon my ears
'Awake my love with joy
today is your Easter Day'

EXULTATION

Glorious bright sun
Dance in exultation
For the Son is risen
Surely as the dawn
Out of the tomb
Back from the dead

Rejoice radiant earth
In this great splendour
Bulbs burst into bloom
Bare trees now blossom
For Christ, Lord of life
Returns from the grave

Rivers ripple with joy
Streams sparkle and shine
The Lord's glory fills you
Darkness vanishes for ever
Let sweet songs fill the skies
He is risen that we might rise

Alleluia! Amen

THE SUN DANCES

There is a lovely tradition from the Hebrides that the sun dances on Easter morning. Behind this is the belief that the whole of creation is changed by the resurrection of Jesus Christ. Not only the human race but every tree, plant, flower, and every creature of the earth, the air, the sea is raised with Christ. We are invited to join the dance of creation and to rejoice in the risen Lord.

'We are Easter people. Alleluia is our song.'[1]

1 Augustine of Hippo

A NEW SPRING

Let the earth proclaim
The joy of your name

Let each bulb rejoice
Its growth be a voice

Let each seed and each flower
Tell of your power

Let the glowing bright sun
Show the deed that is done

Let us hear from the rain
He is risen again

Let all repeat the refrain
He is risen again

ETERNAL SPRING

I do not wait for heaven
I enjoy it all along
It is there in sun and shade
In work as well as song

I do not wait for heaven
I rest there all the way
It is not seen, it is not heard
Yet present in each day

I do not wait for heaven
When the birds begin to sing
God's love is all about us
As we celebrate the spring

I do not wait for heaven
Or for winter to go by
I trust in God's eternal spring
I need not fear to die

I have a vision of a class of children bored out of their minds with the stories of Jesus. Their room is dull and, it seems, so are their lives. Suddenly, the words are heard: 'Here comes the sun!' Then the room fills with light, the faces brighten, the story comes alive. Here is life and vitality.

I move on to a group of theological students all in grey with a grey-faced teacher. They look asleep. The drone of a dull voice dissecting words offers no life. Then the words are heard: 'Here comes the sun!' Colour enters into the room, lightness into the speaker's voice, awakening and attention into the students. Here is the word of life.

I move out, in my vision, to a drab-looking church. The hymns drag and the prayers are not touching the people. The sermon seems far away. Again the words: 'Here comes the sun!' The building is suddenly a blaze of light. Music and prayers reach into hearts. The preacher is direct and the congregation full of life. They will take this light with them into their homes.

Then I hear the words of Isaiah 60 verses 1–3.

Arise, shine out, for your light has come,
The glory of the Lord is rising upon you.
Though night still covers the earth,
And darkness the peoples;
Above you the Holy One arises,
And above you God's glory appears.

I hear the words again but they have a new meaning, they are about the presence of God. I hear: 'Here comes the Son!' This is the presence that transforms all things and people. It is time to take up the challenge set by Gerard Manley Hopkins:

'Let him Easter in us, be a day spring to the dimness of us.'[1]

1 From 'The wreck of the Deutschland'

A FLIGHT OF BIRDS

Lonely is the curlew on the moorland hill
High is the lark when the wind is still
Swift is the hawk that drops on its prey
Dainty is the tit that dances in the may

Happy is the grouse with throaty laughter
Sad is the lapwing that's lost a daughter
Bold is the cuckoo in the dark wood
Proud is the moorhen with her brood

Secret is the owl alone in her nest
Odd is the jay when he calls in jest
Ragged is the starling on the green
Grumpy is the blackbird when it's seen

Sacred is the heron bent over the lake
Cheeky is the robin looking for cake
Mighty is the eagle flying to the sun
He is out of sight. Our flight is done

SUDDENLY

Suddenly the sun came out
From grey and heavy clouds
In a moment the light swept
Over the houses and church
All were transformed

Suddenly the Son broke out
From the darkness of the tomb
In a moment his light swept
Over a distressed woman
Over a disturbed world

EPIPHANIES

Revealed in flesh
To the tug of Joseph
To the breast of Mary

Manifested to the world
Shown to the shepherds
Displayed to the wise men

Exposed to the soldiers
To fists and the whip
To the crown of thorns

Displayed to the crowds
Lifted up on the cross
To weaken and die

Appearing at Easter
First to Mary
Then the disciples

Seen on the shore
The edge of time
Beginning of eternity

ILLUSTRATIONS

Easter Eggs (oil on canvas) by Edward Atkinson Hornel (1864–1933), The Drambuie Collection, Edinburgh, Scotland/ Bridgeman Art Library.

Robin and Sparrow (oil on board) by Fred Cuming (b. 1930), Private Collection/Bridgeman Art Library. Courtesy of Manya Igel Fine Arts Ltd.

Grongar Hill, Carmarthenshire 1944, Illustration from *English, Scottish and Welsh Landscape Verse*, Betjeman and Taylor, 1944 by John Piper (1903–92), Private Collection/Bridgeman Art Library.

Feeding the Lambs by Dorothea Sharp (1874–1955), Beaton-Brown Fine Paintings, London, UK/Bridgeman Art Library. The publisher has been unable to trace the copyright holder and would be grateful to receive any information as to their identity and whereabouts.

Wind and Rain, 1994 (oil on board) by Willie Rodger (Contemporary Artist), Private Collection/Bridgeman Art Library.

Spring Tulips in Bloom at the Keukenhof, Holland by Max Agostini (1914–97), © ADAGP, Paris and DACS, London 2005/ Galerie Martin-Caille Matignon, Paris, France/Bridgeman Art Library.

The Gardener by Sir Alfred Munnings (1878–1959), © The Sir Alfred Munnings Art Museum, Castle House, Dedham, UK/Phillips, The International Fine Art Auctioneers, UK/Bridgeman Art Library.

Spring Has Come by George F. Henry (1858–1943), Smith Art Gallery and Museum, Stirling, Scotland/Bridgeman Art Library. The publisher has been unable to trace the copyright holder and would be grateful to receive any information as to their identity and whereabouts.

Landscape in Schleswig-Holstein by Emil Nolde (1867–1956), © Nolde-Stiftung Seebüll/Stadelsches Kunstinstitut, Frankfurt-am-Main, Germany/Bridgeman Art Library.

Fishing in the Spring, Pont de Clichy, 1887 (oil on canvas) by Vincent van Gogh (1853–90), Art Institute of Chicago, IL, USA/Bridgeman Art Library Giraudon/Bridgeman Art Library.

Christ Clasping the Cross by El Greco (Domenico Theotocopuli) (1541–1614), Prado, Madrid, Spain/Bridgeman Art Library.

Winter Garden, Sunset (oil on canvas) by Fred Cuming (b. 1930), Private Collection/Bridgeman Art Library. Courtesy of Simon Gillespie Studio, London.

Girl Dressing, 1922 (oil on canvas) by Dorothy Johnstone (1892–1980), Private Collection/Bridgeman Art Library. Courtesy of Bourne Fine Art, Edinburgh, Scotland.

The Resurrection, panel from the St Thomas Altar from St John's Church, Hamburg, begun in 1424 (tempera and oil on panel) by Master Francke (*c.* 1385–*c.* 1436), Hamburg Kunsthalle, Hamburg, Germany/Bridgeman Art Library.

The Disciples Peter and John Running to the Sepulchre on the Morning of the Resurrection, c. 1898 (oil on canvas) by Eugene Burnand (1850–1921), Musée d'Orsay, Paris, France/Bridgeman Art Library Lauros/Giraudon/Bridgeman Art Library.

Low Tide, Morston Harbour (oil on canvas) by Hugo Grenville (b. 1958), Private Collection/Bridgeman Art Library.

Pansies and Terracotta Pots (w/c) by Karen Armitage (Contemporary Artist), Private Collection/Bridgeman Art Library.

The Brook by John Singer Sargent (1856–1925), Private Collection/Bridgeman Art Library.

Dawn Walk (oil on board) by Fred Cuming (b. 1930), Private Collection/Bridgeman Art Library. Courtesy of Manya Igel Fine Arts Ltd.

Blue Tit and Milk Bottle, 1982 (oil on canvas) by Peter Wilson (Contemporary Artist), Private Collection/ Bridgeman Art Library.

Before the Hurricane, Regent Street, 1988 (oil on canvas) by Bill Jacklin (Contemporary Artist), Private Collection/ Bridgeman Art Library.

Hell Bay, Late Afternoon (oil on canvas) by Hugo Grenville (b. 1958), Private Collection/Bridgeman Art Library.